The
Knight Life

The
Knight Life

"CHiVaLRY ain't DeaD"

Keith Knight

GRAND CENTRAL
PUBLISHING

New York Boston

Grand Central Publishing
Hachette Book Group
237 Park Avenue
New York, NY 10017
www.HachetteBookGroup.com

Printed in China

First Edition: June 2010

10 9 8 7 6 5 4 3 2 1

Grand Central Publishing is a division of Hachette Book Group, Inc.
The Grand Central Publishing name and logo is a trademark of Hachette Book Group, Inc.

Library of Congress Cataloging-in-Publication Data

ISBN: 978-0-446-54866-3

Library of Congress Control Number: 2009934324

For my family,
with love.

Acknowledgments

Thanks to Ted Rall and the folks at United Media for getting the ball rolling with the strip—especially Reed Jackson and Mikhaela Reid; Marc Gerald and the Agency Group; Karen, Latoya, and the gang at Grand Central; all the papers that run the strip; my faithful readers; and, most of all, thanks to my family, both here and abroad, for allowing me to make fun of you. Especially Pops and my lovely, lovely über-wife, Kerstin.

Uncle, we miss you already.

Foreword

Teen Michael Jackson impersonator, guerrilla marketing expert, bohemian rap CD legend—Keith Knight has been all these things. But the greatest of his titles has been cartoonist.

Vividly I remember Keith—or "Keef," as he is affectionately known to his publishers—changing the game by striding majestically through media conventions while humming "I'm Bad," wearing sandwich boards and nothing else. (The signage read: "Buy this book or the sheep gets it…again." Did he sell books? Do Bay Area denizens love nudity and sheep?) Not for nothing did the *San Francisco Chronicle* call him "the coolest person in San Francisco." (He moved to L.A. shortly thereafter.) Could Keith do anything cooler?

Yes, he could. There had been *The K Chronicles* and "(th)Ink" and cartoons in magazines like *ESPN* and *Mad*. There had been eight books, including an omnibus anthology, *The K Chronicles*.

But to Keef fans who would no longer have to wait a week or more to get their fix of his quirky humor, the May 5, 2008, debut of *The Knight Life* was indeed the coolest development since the day that cat Theodore scratched. And now, here in your bacon-greased hands, is Mr. Knight's first collection of his daily syndicated strip.

This is the point at which I am supposed to tell you about the terrible struggle of the artist to express his true inner vision. So, OK. They told him he should carefully focus the daily strip. But no. More Keef more of the time meant more, more, more.

Within weeks, we had seen him conduct an inquiry into extraterrestrial racism and offer parenting lessons with Dexter the gangsta rapper. We got airline passengers from hell, '80s Europop and Nelly Furtado. We saw cheap left-wing editors and passive-aggro L.A. café culture exposed. And then, because 2008 was just *like that*, it got even weirder: Recession! Budget cuts! War vets! Real estate follies! Health insurance! Emo-poets! Mexican Coke! Hippie infestations! And somehow *The Knight Life*—without being topical—captured the kablammo mania of it all.

Keith figured that if *The K Chronicles* was his blog, *The Knight Life* was his network sitcom. In Keith's version, everyone in the production crew was written into the script. Or, more precisely, *drawn* into the script, in that trademark slurpy noodle, Johnny Hart-slacker, polycultural-Peter Bagge, Plastic Man-gets-funky-without-any-arms style.

They told him he should limit the strip to four characters or less in the first year. Instead, aside from him and Kerstin, his equally bug-eyed-at-the-world wife, we got their best friends Clovis the Dreaded and Gunther the Doomed; Keef's low-rolling dad and Kerstin's currency-hedging brother; Dexter and overachieving Lil Dex; Pudge the college roommate; the Leftie Guy, the Cubicle Guy, LAPD, Techie Becky, over-brewed Stew, and Barnaby the Memoirist, among many more. Is this the biggest, weirdest, most diverse group of characters ever seen on the funny pages in the first year of a strip? Maybe, probably, I have no idea.

But WOW, what a beginning. Days like this that we're going through, it's never certain that your or my life will get any better, but we know that *The Knight Life* certainly will. In the meantime and forever—let us raise a toast to the small thorough-going satisfaction of Life's Little Victories.

Jeff Chang
Berkeley, CA
November 2009

The
Knight Life

▲1984: I was the official MJ impersonator for Jordan Marsh, a department store in Boston.

▲Since this first episode, Kerstin/Spider strips have become a reader favorite.

▲This strip was based on when my dad took the family to see *Papillon* at the drive-in.

▲This gag doesn't work anymore.

▲That's a Washington Generals flag I got there.

▲A cat named Theodore really did invent scratching: Grand Wizard Theodore.

▲Gunther began the strip naked. The syndicate suggested I put clothes on him.

▲I was informed that my comics were the most stolen item out of the library at the local juvie hall.

▲Supermodels only date cartoonists. It's the industry's dirty little secret.

▲ This tree is in Santa Barbara.

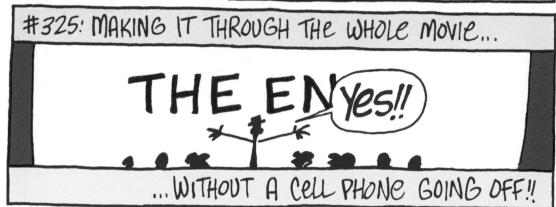

▲ "Life's Little Victories" is a series I started with my alt-weekly strip, *The K Chronicles*. People love 'em.

▲I was accused of being a racist with this one.

▲My favorite. BTW: That's a basketball in the last panel, not a watermelon.

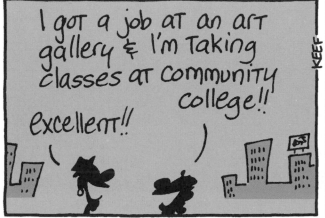

▲A-ha, Kajagoogoo, and the Human League, respectively.

SHOPPING FOR A NEW MATTRESS

This one is incredibly soft.

It's made of 100% Peruvian Yak hair!!

Whoa... Maybe it's a little **Too** soft.

It's softer than a Will Smith rap song!!

I'm gonna need a little help getting out of this thing...

That'll be a $15 surcharge.

SHOPPING FOR A NEW MATTRESS

This one is too hard.

This concrete model is our best-selling product.

Why would anyone want to sleep on a slab of concrete?

It's very popular with the urban trendy set. It allows them to feel what it's like to be homeless!!

Why pay $5,000 when you can go sleep on the street for free?

To feel homeless in the safety of your own home!!

SHOPPING FOR A NEW MATTRESS

Ooo!! Now **This** mattress is perfect!!

Ah, yes.. Our hot seller from Japan. We only have one.

Reviewers call it "The last mattress you'll ever need."

Nice!!

Mainly because the purchaser mysteriously dies 7 days after bringing it home.

▲An homage to the Japanese horror classic *Ringu*.

▲Dexter Sr. represents all those guys who bullied me in school.

▲Poof!! There goes my guest appearance on *Oprah*.

▲The traffic stop has since become a regular set-up between these two characters.

Do you think any birds will use the birdhouse I put up?

Why not?

Like that old Kevin Costner movie sez: "If you build it, they will come."

PLOP

And when they come, they will leave droppings.

TWEET TWEET TWEET TWEET

!

Tweedle TWEET TWEET

Darling!! Wake up!! Listen!! Do you know what that means?

BANG

Time to move to a new neighborhood?

You look ghastly.

Someone's been lighting firecrackers outside my bedroom window.

I never understood the appeal of firecrackers.

They're not visual. It's just **noise**.

Yeah...

BUT tape a few to your sister's Barbies, and you've got adolescent gold!!

LET'S CELEBRATE MORE OF...

LiFe's LiTTLe VicToRieS

YeS!!

#1326: GRABBING A HANDFUL OF QUARTERS OUT OF THE CHANGE JAR..

Scrounge rummage scrape

..AND IT'S **JUST ENOUGH** TO FINISH THE LAUNDRY!!!

Last one!!

Perfect!! YeS!!

KEEF

7/6

theknightlifecomic@yahoo.com

#1327: FINDING **$10** IN AN OLD PAIR OF JEANS!!

JORDache!!

YeS!!

©2008 K. Knight/Dist. by UFS, Inc.

#1328: GETTING YER STUFF OUTTA THE DRYER...

THANK YOU, LAUNDRY GODS!!

AND THERE'RE **NO ORPHANED SOCKS!!**

www.comics.com

#1329: **FINALLY** SEEING THE BOTTOM OF YOUR DIRTY LAUNDRY HAMPER!!

YEEEESSSSS

▲A real, authentic tag from my hood!!

Gym Class Heroes. Reel Big Fish...

Relient K MC Chris. Shwayze.

That ain't so bad. I still got a few years left.

Whaddaya mean?

I've heard of 5 of the 80 bands on this year's Warped Tour!!

I read that a black man's life expectancy is 10 years shorter than almost everyone else's!!

Not in prison!!

Come again?

Statistically, the black prison population has a longer life span than the general black populace.

Uh, no thanks.

C'mon!! It's for your own good!!

What's up with cherry-flavored cranberries?

Why make a fruit taste like another fruit?

There aren't apple-flavored bananas or kiwi-flavored kumquats.

I want my cranberries to taste like cranberries. Is that too much to ask?

Know what I buy when I want the taste of cherries?

Ummm... Cherries?

Yup. They taste just like 'em!!

▲A favorite.

▲Have you seen what they offer at The Learning Annex? Weird.

This is the pool? Isn't it too shallow to swim in?

Don't trust your eyes. They can deceive you.

How will I learn to swim in here?

SHADDUP & GET IN!!

Whoa. Deceptively deep.

Like a Nelly Furtado song!!

That guy is pale & bloated. Is he okay?

That's the most convincing "Dead Man's float" I've ever seen!!

Should we pull him out?

And mess with perfection? Are you crazy?!!

▲Floating corpse: Comic gold!!

AT THE LEARNING ANNEX

How was your swimming class?

All wet.

The instructor claimed to be half dolphin & said he was here for a higher porpoise!!

Men in white coats took him away in a tuna net.

How did your waterboarding class go?

Ugh, torturous!!

Keef.. Did you know your comics in the paper are missing punch lines?

They're supposed to be like that.

To get the punch lines, you have to go to the web site & pay a membership fee.

©2008 K. Knight/Dist. by UFS, Inc.

Or you can call a 1-900 number. You'll hear me say the joke for just $2.99!!

www.comics.com

If you're rich, you can pay $800 & I'll come to your house & draw it right in your paper--live, in person!!

KEEF

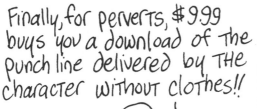

Finally, for perverts, $9.99 buys you a download of the punch line delivered by the character without clothes!!

keef@knightlifecomic.com

You've sure got all the bases covered.

Uncovered. That's why they're called comic "strips".

Payment will be automatically deducted from your bank account

7/27

▲Two naked black men on the comics page? What progress America has made!!

THIS is why I could never work in a supermarket.

▲When my fish guy sees this, he's gonna hate me.

▲I didn't know what a durian was 'til my editor told me.

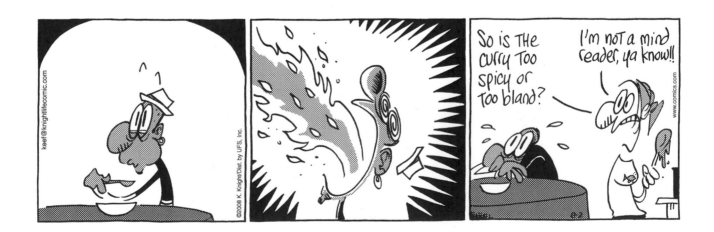

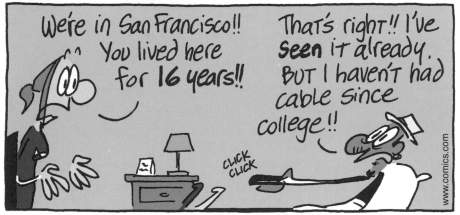

▲This one is dedicated to everyone trying to make a living as a cartoonist.

STOP!! You can't use Luke Skywalker to pay The credit card bill!!

90% of our mail is bills. We're out of Vaders & StormTroopers.

We'll have To buy another sheet.

8/7

THE TROUBLE WITH STAR WARS STAMPS

How 'bout Han & Chewie for your old roommate's birthday?

Are you crazy? His wife has a mustache!!

KEEF

©2008 K. Knight/Dist. by UFS, Inc.

Darling.. There's gonna be a lot of free food floating around this art gallery opening.

Grab whatever They're offering, okay?

BUT I am!!

But I'm not hungry.

The best Thing about marriage is gaining an extra pair of eyes & hands for scoring free food!!

Like a roach?

8/8

KEEF

keef@knightlifecomic.com

www.knightlifecomic.com

www.comics.com

©2008 K. Knight/Dist. by UFS, Inc.

What are you doing?

Celebrating The miracle of life.

I've OD'ed on **death** Today. On TV. In The newspaper. AT The movies. I've seen Too many people dying.

I need some **balance**. So I'm celebrating The miracle of life!!

8/9

You're staring at mildew growing on The shower curtain.

Life is where you find it.

KEEF

www.comics.com

©2008 K. Knight/Dist. by UFS, Inc.

▲My dad has more plastic bags than a landfill.

▲Our local hardware store went out of business after ninety-five years.

How'd you like your first visit to Home Repo?

It was truly enlightening.

Men from all walks of life, coming together in an amalgamation of **steel**, **wood**, **nuts** & **bolts**!!

8-14

Cops. Plumbers. Truckers. Day Laborers. Construction Workers.

It was like a Village People video.

KEEF

keef@knightlifecomic.com   www.comics.com

Clovis!! How deep do you want me to dig?

Two feet!!

COMING SOON

COMMUNITY GARDEN

www.knightlifecomic.com

Two feet? Isn't that a bit much?

I--I didn't m-mean two feet... I m-meant--

keef@knightlifecomic.com

T-two f-feet!!

oh.

www.comics.com

8-15

They look like human feet, all right.

You dug them up?

keef@knightlifecomic.com   ©2008 K. Knight/Dist. by UFS, Inc.

8-16

Welp. You can never be too careful. **YOU'RE ALL SUSPECTS!!**

www.comics.com

You were **SO** right!! Starting a community garden **did** bring us all closer together!!

POLICE

©2008 K. Knight/Dist. by UFS, Inc.

Keith..What's wrong with Gunther?

Some novelty web site says he's gonna die next week.

He knows it's not true. Right?

He's taking it pretty seriously.

Maybe it'll light a fire under his butt to accomplish some longstanding goal.

Time ticking away..must try that shrimp plate at Applebee's.

I can't believe I only have one week to live!!

Dude..we all gotta go sometime!!

It isn't fair!!

Sure it is!! Death is the ultimate equalizer!!

BUT I JUST STOCKED UP ON A TON OF STUFF FROM COSTCO!!

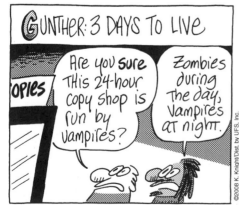

GUNTHER: 3 DAYS TO LIVE

Are you **sure** this 24-hour copy shop is run by vampires?

Zombies during the day, vampires at night.

And a bite from these folks & I'll live past 3 days?

You'll live past **3,000 years!!**

And wearing these pheromones will attract them to me?

They're not pheromones. It's A1 steak sauce.

▲Copy Crüe? I'd work for them.

▲We trade off delivering the State of the Union. Kerstin's turn next year.

▲Forever stamps were the only investment I made that didn't lose $$$.

▲Gunther is a glutton for punishment.

There you are, scrubbing & cleaning the apartment...
...while I get paid to draw cartoons.
I feel guilty.
9-1

You **COULD** clean the bathroom.
And like that, the guilt is gone!!

What's that?
An article about postwar mentoring.

Old vets are taking young vets under their wings to show them the ropes.

The best eats are in cans behind the French & Middle Eastern places!!
9-2

VET MENTORING
The hardest thing about going to war was coming home.

Upon return, I faced indifference, mistreatment... even open hostility!!
9-3

I got no appreciation for the sacrifice I made for this country.
Protestors can be pretty harsh.

Protestors? I'm talking about the U.S. government!!

Why is a young vet like you on the street?

I have a place to stay.

VET PLS HELP

I nearly got into a car accident on the way back from my shrink. I got out to walk off my frustration.

This driver was on the phone, watching a DVD, weaving in & out of traffic in a huge vehicle!!

I didn't survive 3 tours in Iraq to get killed by a Hummer here at home!!

Word!!

KEEF

9-4

I used to make fun of vets like you.

VET Please Help

I thought vets who couldn't make it in civilian life were **soft** & **weak**.

But after coming back from Iraq & seeing how tough it is -- even with a support system.

I'm sorry.

I **DO** get teary-eyed every time I hear that sad James Blunt song.

VET Please Help

KEEF

9-5

From one vet to another, thanks for mentoring me.

I'm always here for you. 'Cept on Tuesdays.

What's on Tuesday?

I scored a fashion consulting gig for a coupla shops on Melrose.

Are you serious?

"Shabby Chic," bro. Somebody's gotta dress those rock stars!!

KEEF

9-6

▲ Got some great feedback from the "Vet Mentoring" storyline.

Uh-oh. See that dude getting on the bus?

Yup.

He rants maniacally, sending spittle in all directions...

And smells like sweaty ham!!

If we make goofy faces, he'll avoid sitting next to us.

9/7

keef@knightlifecomic.com

©2008 K. Knight/Dist. by UFS, Inc.

www.knightlifecomic.com

HEY YOU NUTJOBS!! GET OFFA MY BUS!! YOU'RE SCARING THE PASSENGERS!!

www.comics.com

At least we're not sitting next to the weird guy!!

▲ Had to change "crackheads" to "nutjobs."

Son.. The first thing you need to become a great playground basketball player is the proper footwear.

These are **Titanium Astro 560**s, the finest sneakers in the biz.

Try 'em on!!

These are gigantic!!

Really?

Hey!! Whaddaya know? They fit **Me**!!

KEEF

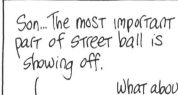
Son... The most important part of street ball is showing off.

What about fundamentals?

WHAT DID YOU JUST SAY?

9-9

What about fundamentals: Dribbling, passing & free throws?

If I **ever** hear you use the "F" word again, you're **grounded for a week!!**

KEEF

Son.. Fundamentalism is what's ruining basketball in America!!

Americans go overseas, teaching foreigners how to dribble, pass & shoot free throws!!

9-10

Now it's coming back to bite America on its oversized bottom!!

Still blaming Europeans for taking the NBA slot that is rightfully yours?

At least Mexicans take jobs none of us want!!

KEEF

▲Don't tell anyone, but I put the word *bong* in a comic strip.

▲My homage to *Misery*.

▲I don't think anyone noticed the "Terminal C" pointing at my character.

▲I'm shocked they allowed me to use "hell." Shocked, I tell you.

It's all about The name.

What?

Success!! It's all about the name!! Take St. John's Wort.

=Bleah= I don't Think so...

You should!! It's good for you!!

It sounds like it was harvested from a pus-filled growth.

©2008 K. Knight/Dist. by UFS, Inc.

I'd change The name To Salmonella.

Salmonella? The bacteria That causes food poisoning?

www.knightlifecomic.com

www.comics.com

9-21

Salmonella's too cool a word to waste on something bad... Sort of like "Spina Bifida" & "Janjaweed".

It does sound like a delicious lox-filled spread for bagels.

KEEF

▲ Catching "St. John's wort" sounds worse than salmonella. And I will never use pink for a background again!!

Strip 1 (9-22):

Yep?

Pete!! Please hold onto this box of plastic bags for me.

What for?

My son wants me to recycle them, but I'm a plastic bag junkie!!

Just hold 'em till he leaves. I'll be back to pick them up.

Thanks!!

Back in my day, it used to be a box of dirty books.

What has society come to?

Strip 2 (9-23): VISITING MY DAD

I'm gonna sleep another hour.

Isn't ten enough?!!

Pops. The older I get, the longer I sleep.

I hope to work it up to 23 hours a night in my final days.

That way when I die, I'll be used to it.

Whatever happened to you, I blame your mother.

Strip 3 (9-24): MEETING DAD'S CASINO BUDS

Hey Pete. Meet my kid.

Oh yeah!! The Bingo Carnie Clown from California.

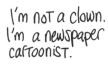

I'm not a clown. I'm a newspaper cartoonist.

I'm old, not deaf. Your Dad said: Bingo Carnie Clown.

"Bingo Carnie Clown"?

I was just trying to make you sound more dignified!!

▲Nothing said "back to school" for me more than the Mead Trapper Keeper.

▲The "brick" wall looks terrible.

Class, due to school budget cuts, the letter "K" will be deleted from the alphabet.

ABCDEFGHIJLM

10-2

The letter "C" will be used to pic up the slac.

Any questions?

Good. Because we're phasing out the question marc, too.

ABCDEFC

Your school is phasing out the letter "K"? What for?

Budget cuts.

What will folks with "K" names do?

How will we score strikeouts in baseball games?

On the other hand, there'll be no more K.K.K.!!

If only it were that easy.

10-3

Ma'am, I object to your dropping the letter "K" from the alphabet.

PRINCIPAL'S OFFICE

It'll save us 500K over the next fiscal year!!

How can you expect your students to compete if you don't teach them the whole alphabet?

Have you seen the way youth write these days? LOL!!

"K" is redundant!! "C" can cover for it.

PRINCIPAL

10-4

This is **not** okay!!

No. It's "O.C."

PRINCIPAL

▲▼A couple of favorites.

WHAT ARE **YOU** DOING TO SURVIVE THE RECESSION?

I went on "Antiques Roadshow" to see what I could get for this **old relic** I found sitting in my attic.

But they told me I probably couldn't get much for him.

WHERE'S MY BOURBON?

I'm gonna try craigslist.

WHAT ARE **YOU** DOING TO SAVE MONEY?

I'm taking my bike to work every day--

--BUT I don't think it's helping...

The stupid thing barely fits in the trunk of my car!!

RECESSION MOVIE NIGHT

Slender pickings in the library's DVD section.

Score anything?

"Shine a Light," Martin Scorsese's Rolling Stones concert film.

ROLLING STONES SHINE A LIGHT

Also "Young at Heart." It's a doc about a group of seniors that sing classic rock songs.

You got the same movie twice?

▲Surprised this made it through.

▲The best thing about getting married is having a whole new family to make fun of.

Excuse me. Where is my husband?

Come again?

Since my parents arrived from Germany, an imposter has taken his place!!

This imposter cooks, cleans, does laundry... He even folds my Mom's underwear!!

Sounds like your husband To me.

You're the biggest brown-noser I've ever met!!

This brown is natural, baby.

10-16

There are two Bentleys in our driveway.

They're my brother's. He just got them.

I know The Euro is strong against the dollar. But don't you think he's going a little overboard?

He doesn't know how long our weak dollar will last.

10-17

He's hired Kanye West To play our backyard BBQ.

That IS strange. He likes Jay-Z better!!

Kanye West Sat, Keefs

KEEF

▲ Second panel: a rare ¾ position. Now you see why I don't do it more.

KERSTIN'S FAMILY LEAVES

Are you okay?

I always feel like I'll never see them again.

My Dad is 70. He's not getting any younger.

SECU

He's been doing yoga every day for 40 years. He started boogie boarding at 69!!

10-18

You should worry That he'll outlive us!!

GATES

KEEF

NOW, MORE THAN EVER... celebrate LIFE'S LITTLE VICTORIES

©2008 K. Knight/Dist. by UFS, Inc.

#2108: HAVING **NO CASH** FOR FOOD...

=SIGH=

THE "Brando" $7

10/19

..WHEN A FRIEND SHOWS UP WHO **OWES YOU MONEY!!**

Hey KEITH!! Here's That Ten I owe ya.

Yes!!

#2109: AN **EXTRA** CANDY BAR...

CHOCO CRACK

CHOCO CRACK

KEEF

www.comics.com

..FALLS OUT OF THE VENDING MACHINE!!

#2110: INSTEAD OF A PRICEY PRESCRIPTION...

Yes!!

..YOUR DOC GIVES YOU A BUNCH OF **FREE SAMPLES!!**

#2111: FINDING AN **ICE CREAM** IN THE BACK OF THE FREEZER THAT YOU FORGOT ABOUT!!

Yes!!

#2112: ARRIVING TO WORK **SUPER LATE**...

I am SO Fired!!

..AND YOUR BOSS ARRIVES **TEN MINUTES LATER!!**

AHA!! WHERE HAVE YOU BEEN?!!

heh.

▲Mmmm . . . taco truck!!

▲Originally my character wore a different hat. I had to redraw the hat in dozens of strips. In this one, that hat is *way* too small.

This new high-end cinema experience is great!!

Nice!!

Cushy seats!! Tasty cocktails!! High-brow eats & great service!!

Excellent!!

And that full-body massage I got halfway through the film was exquisite!!

Sir... we don't give massages.

10-30

My mom's been talking to me about real estate.

Start with a decent down payment..

And stay away from those adjustable rate mortgages..

10-31

I KNOW IT'S IMPORTANT TO KNOW THIS STUFF... AND I TRY MY BEST TO PAY ATTENTION.

When you apply for insurance...

make sure you raise your deductible..

BUT AFTER ABOUT A MINUTE & A HALF...

Thoroughly inspect the place before you even THINK about signing.

IT ALL SOUNDS GREEK TO ME.

Alpha Beta Mousaka Soccates Sigma PHI Souvlaki
ΔΣΠ
Acropolis...

Do you constantly find yourself breathing?

Then you should try Morontia™!!

Taking Morontia™ 3 times a day has been **clinically proven** not to affect normal breathing patterns in an overly adverse way.

Ask your doctor about Morontia™!!

11-1

Side effects include continued Pharmaceutical company profits, empty wallets & the mockery & condescension of others for falling for stupid ads like this.

Did ya hear? They're trying to pass a law against dogs on drivers' laps!!

If they pass that law, I'm as good as **DEAD.**

What do you mean?

My car's **old!!** I don't have airbags!!

Mr. Yentl is my Doggie-Bag!!

KEEF

©2008 K. Knight/Dist. by UFS, Inc.
www.comics.com

11-3

After your record company faked your death, you ever worry someone would recognize you on the street?

Hey!!

11-4

Ohmigosh!! You look just like that famous rapper!! What's-his-name...

keef@knightlifecomic.com

WHAT?!! ARE YOU SAYIN' ALL BLACK FOLKS LOOK ALIKE?!!

Whoops... Sorry, bra...

©2008 K. Knight/Dist. by UFS, Inc.

I manage.

KEEF

www.comics.com

THIS DUDE ON THE BUS WAS PICKING HIS NOSE.

Dig Dig

Grind

AFTER 15 MINUTES, I **HAD** TO SAY SOMETHING.

Good gracious, man. How deep can you go?

Dig Grind

Search

11-5

©2008 K. Knight/Dist. by UFS, Inc.
www.comics.com

HE DIDN'T STOP 'TIL HE PULLED OUT A COAL MINER.

There're six more of us in there!!

▲ I like the weird ones.

▲ Guaranteed to be the only strip that references obscure Andy Warhol films.

A CONVERSATION I HAD IN A LONDON PUB.

TEACH THE BLOODY SPROGS HOW TO **STAB**!!

Ye olde Puke & Vomit Pub

I'll tell ya how to get the guns away from American kids, mate!!

www.knightlifecomic.com

'ear me out, mate!! A gun is a **coward's** weapon, it is...

KEEF.

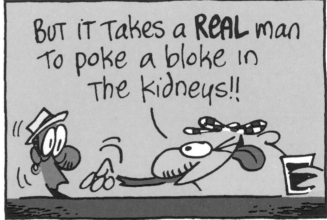

BUT IT takes a **REAL** man to poke a bloke in the kidneys!!

When was the last time you heard of someone killed by a drive-by stabbing?

www.comics.com

©2008 K. Knight/Dist. by UFS, Inc.

11-9

In a bizarre & twisted way, you have a point.

And a bloody sharp one at that, mate!!

▲A reader wanted to boycott all newspapers that carried my strip because I used "puke" and "vomit" as the name of a pub. No mention of teaching kids how to stab.

▲I've always wondered about *Hogan's Heroes* in Germany.

▲Surprised this made it through.

Celebrate B-4 it's 2 Late!! Life's Little Victories

#1008: GOING THRU THE GROCERY CHECKOUT LINE WITH **ORGANIC** PRODUCE...

Yes!!

..& GETTING CHARGED FOR THE **CHEAP, ORDINARY** KIND!!

#1009: A **SLOWPOKE** CUTS IN FRONT OF YOU ON THE FREEWAY...

!@☆#!!

...JUST BEFORE PASSING A **COP** WITH A **RADAR GUN!**

Yes!!

#1010: HAVING THE **EXACT** NUMBER OF HANGERS NEEDED FOR THE FRESH LAUNDRY!!

Yes!!

11/16

©2008 K. Knight/Dist. by UFS, Inc.

www.comics.com

#1011: THOSE **GIGANTIC PILLS** YOUR DOCTOR PRESCRIBED...

GULP

Yes!!

..GO DOWN EASY!!

keef@knightlifecomic.com

#1012: FINDING THAT **HOT NEW** BOOK -- ON THE **STREET** FOR **SUPER CHEAP!!**

50¢ & IT'S YOURS!!

MY NEW BOOK!!

COMIX BY KEEF

Uh... YES?

KEEF

▲ I was accused by a reader of corrupting children because I didn't go back and pay full price for the organic produce.

PERPETUALLY PREGNANT PEGGY

The twins came first.

We figured the next time would only get easier. But then I had **quadruplets!!**

We're hoping for just triplets this time. And maybe a single after that.

In baseball, it's called "hitting for the cycle"!!

11-17

PERPETUALLY PREGNANT PEGGY

You named your kids after soft drinks?

I hope they get sponsored.

My bickering twins are called Coke & Pepsi. The little one is Sprite. The manic one is Mountain Dew.

Last but not least, is Mr. Pibb.

11-18

I don't see him.

Mr. Pibb is always the hardest to find.

PERPETUALLY PREGNANT PEGGY

You really think beverage companies will sponsor your kids because you named them after soft drinks?

We've already received free logo-covered schwag!!

It's a win-win. We get free stuff & the corporations have ad space for life!!

Isn't that unhealthy for the kids?

11-19

Oh no.. It's inspirational!!

Dr Pepper wants to be a **real doctor** when she grows up!!

>BURP<

They're so **creepy.**

One was crawling across my Mom's kitchen floor. I **freaked.**

They were everywhere, dude!! If we don't do something, they're gonna take over!!

Gunther met his brother's twins for the first time.

Check out that dude, Keef. Look at that parasite attached to him.

What was once a man with hopes & dreams is now a mere **zombie.**

His life-force slowly sucked out of him, night after sleepless night, by that nocturnal creature!!

SUCK SUCK

Toothless vampires!! That's what babies **really** are!!

I don't know why folks get so flustered about illegal immigration. There's a much bigger baby problem!!

Babies don't **work.** They don't pay **taxes.** They don't speak our **language.**

You were once a baby too, Gunther.

BUT I GREW OUT OF IT!!

When are they gonna expand our cubicles?

What are you talking about?

There's a new law. It says our workspaces have to be big enough for us to lie down, stand up, fully extend our limbs & turn around freely.

11-24

That law is for **livestock.** You know, cows. pigs. chickens.

Really?

©2008 K. Knight/Dist. by UFS, Inc.
keef@knightlifecomic.com

Maybe I can get my campaign contribution back.

www.comics.com

KEEF

Yo, Cartoon Man!! I want you to illustrate the cover of my first book!!

What is it?

Urban fiction. It's about a legendary gangsta rapper & his struggles to get his **brilliant** first book published--

11-25

keef@knightlifecomic.com
www.comics.com

.. and the cartoonist whose **face** he **smashes** because said cartoonist refused to draw the cover!!

©2008 K. Knight/Dist. by UFS, Inc.
www.comics.com

Sounds like non-fiction, except for the cartoonist with the smashed face.

Fiction or Non-fiction. Your choice.

KEEF

⊳DRAWING THE COVER OF DEXTER'S NEW BOOK

Put me in a diaper on the cover, surrounded by pit bulls & body bags...

www.comics.com

CAFE

...with women in thongs holding AK-47s & machetes.

≋Sigh≋ Why not put the dogs in thongs & the women on leashes?

11-26

©2008 K. Knight/Dist. by UFS, Inc.

Wow. You're a mind-reader!! But I thought it might be too much for a children's book.

Children's book?!!

keef@knightlifecomic.com   KEEF

▲Kerstin's shirt became darker after the syndicate thought she looked nude in a white shirt.

▲Clarence has a different instrument every time.

Panel 1: I HAVE AN EVIL TWIN SISTER

I am **NOT** EVIL!!

©2008 K. Knight/Dist. by UFS, Inc.

Panel 2: WE ARE EXACT OPPOSITES

Male
Slouchy
Drinks Tea in L.A.
Leftie

Female
Perky
Sells Tea in Seattle
Rightie

T(ea) gallery

12-1

Panel 3: TECHNICALLY, I'M 9 MINUTES OLDER. SOMETHING I NEVER LET HER FORGET.

I don't get this cartoon.

You'll get it in about 9 minutes or so.

www.comics.com

KEEF

Panel 4: FOLKS OFTEN ASK HOW LONG I'VE BEEN DRAWING...

I TELL 'EM I WAS **BORN** WITH A MARKER IN MY HAND!!

©2008 K. Knight/Dist. by UFS, Inc.

12-2

Panel 5: WHICH EXPLAINS WHY MY TWIN SIS WAS BORN WITH A TWIRLY MUSTACHE...

...AND A TIC-TAC-TOE GAME ON HER BOTTOM.

www.comics.com

Panel 6: MY EVIL TWIN SISTER'S DOG WANTS TO KILL ME.

GRRRRRRRRRR

VICIOUS COCKER SPANIEL?!!

www.comics.com

Panel 7: I'M SERIOUS!! WHEN I VISIT, SHE HAS TO LOCK THE BRUTE IN A TITANIUM STEEL-REINFORCED CAGE...

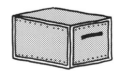

HANNIBAL LECTER STYLE

Panel 8: I WONDER WHAT HE SEES WHEN HE LOOKS AT ME.

BARK BARK BARK

Hi, Buddy!!

©2008 K. Knight/Dist. by UFS, Inc.

12-3

12-7

▲Someone wrote to say how stupid I was for spelling "old" wrong.

▲My wife cheats—*and* she beats me.

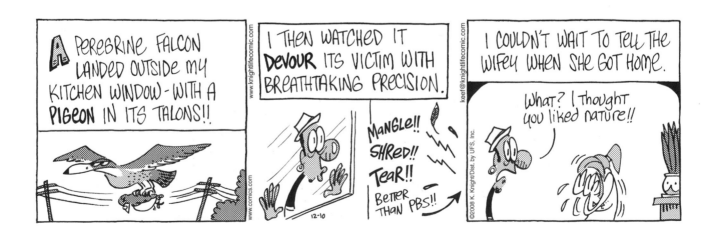

Strip 1 (12-11):

TEACHING THE CHILDREN

Kids, Martin Luther King's appeal was rooted in nonviolence!!

We as a people must never stray from that principle!!

SLAM

©2008 K. Knight/Dist. by UFS, Inc.

Except, of course, when mosquitoes are concerned.

KEEF

www.comics.com

keef@knightlifecomic.com

Strip 2 (12-12):

How is donating blood my patriotic obligation?

Consider all the blood that's been spilled in the name of "freedom" & "democracy."

www.comics.com
www.knightlifecomic.com

We should donate AT least a pint for every 3 months this war goes on!!

Hemoglobin offsets. You may have something there.

Better red than dead!!

©2008 K. Knight/Dist. by UFS, Inc.

keef@knightlifecomic.com

▲Readers are quick to point out they still don't allow gay men to donate blood.

Strip 3 (12-13):

I USED TO WORK AT A YOUTH HOSTEL.

Wait a sec. Is this like the hostel in that movie?

I STILL VOLUNTEER FROM TIME TO TIME.

You know the movie. Where frat boys are enticed by sexy, nubile foreigners to a hostel in eastern europe?

www.comics.com

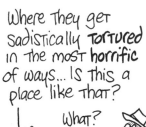

Where they get sadistically TORTURED in the most horrific of ways... Is this a place like that?

What? Heck no!!

©2008 K. Knight/Dist. by UFS, Inc.

Rats.

▲January 20th: Farewell to G. W. Bush/Cheney.

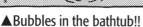

▲Bubbles in the bathtub!!

Everyone I know has adjusted their lifestyle to accommodate the economic downturn.

©2008 K. Knight/Dist. by UFS, Inc.

keef@knightlifecomic.com

MY DAD SWITCHED FROM THE NICKEL SLOTS TO THE PENNY SLOTS...

5X the fun!!

Wall St.

12-21

TECHIE BECKY IS HOLDING OFF ON BUYING THE LATEST GADGET.

How can I **LIVE** unless I have a phone that takes **pix**, bakes **cookies** & performs **angioplasty!!**

MS. HANVEY GOT RID OF HER CAR

DEXTER IS TEACHING

Welcome to the Learning Annex. This class is "how to be a THUG."

WOOF WOOF W

GUNTHER HAS VOLUNTEERED AT THE UNIVERSITY

You're gonna stick WHAT, WHERE?

LAB

You hafta earn those $25!!

KEEF

www.comics.com

▲ One of my favorites.

▲This series really got people into the Dexter character.

▲ This will be the end of *The Knight Life New Year's Eve Television Special!*

▲Gunther's boobs were extremely reduced for the newspaper.

THE WIFEY SCORED A PART-TIME GIG PROMOTING ORGANIC PRODUCE.
I have a Master's Degree in German & English LIT!!
IT'S ALL SHE COULD FIND IN THIS UGLY ECONOMY
I speak 3 languages fluently!!
WHAT LITTLE DIGNITY WAS LEFT SLIPPED AWAY WHEN SHE STEPPED ON A BANANA PEEL.
AUGH!!
©2009 K. Knight/Dist. by UFS, Inc.
www.comics.com
KEEF
1-5

THE WIFEY'S NEW JOB IS STRESSFUL
Shouldn't you be eating healthier, dressed like that?
FEH!! Mind your own beeswax!!
keef@knightlifecomic.com
1-6
Yeesh.. Talk about sour grapes.
If I wanted some WHINE, I'd make some myself!!
©2009 K. Knight/Dist. by UFS, Inc.
www.comics.com
KEEF

▲Giving the wifey a hard time in the strip is fun!

Hey kid. You gotta help me. I've been trying to give away apples all day.
I'll take one!!
www.knightlifecomic.com
keef@knightlifecomic.com
www.comics.com
You will?
Sure!! And my friends will too!!
©2009 K. Knight/Dist. by UFS, Inc.
Wow!! Maybe there is hope for this nation's health!!
Hey everybody! Free computers!!
KEEF
1-7

▲Gunther is a corporate-sponsored air-guitarist.

▲I finish the clown makeup series later in the book.

▲Shout-out to Gary Coleman.

No wonder I haven't seen you lately-- You're no longer homeless!!

For the time being.

As soon as the bank sells it, I'll move.

Will you squat another place?

It's not squatting!! It's a unique program that matches homeless people with people-less homes!!

It's not a government program, is it?

Are you kidding? It makes too much sense!!

▲Three cheers for squatters!!

Some squatters took over the foreclosed place next door!!

Since moving in, they've cleaned up the place. Planted a garden. Hung some art.

And now the drug dealers don't use it anymore!!

THERE GOES THE NEIGHBORHOOD!!

Can you believe it, Keith?

Twenty years ago, I was squatting empty buildings on Avenue C in the Lower East Side!!

Now I'm squatting a 2 bedroom, 2 bathroom house way out in the 'burbs!!

FORECLOSED

I'm fat, old & boring, aren't I?

There, there, Spike. You're living the American dream!!

"CHiVaLRY ain't DeaD" 109

▲No spider is ever harmed in *The Knight Life*. Unlike that fascist, *Garfield*.

Revenge of Life's =Little= VICTORIES

#99: TAKING YOUR CAR IN FOR REPAIR...

JUST in TIME!!

YES!!

..AND FINDING OUT IT'S COVERED BY A WARRANTY YOU THOUGHT HAD EXPIRED!!

©2009 K. Knight/Dist. by UFS, Inc.

#100: STAYING HOME SICK WITH THE FLU & RECEIVING THAT LONG-AWAITED DVD SET IN THE MAIL!!

YES!!

Gamera Collection

KEEF

#101: THE PUBLIC RADIO STATION ENDS ITS FUND DRIVE A WEEK EARLY!!

STOP Sending Money!! We're FLUSH WITH CASH!!*

WHA--?!! YES!!

(*THIS NEVER HAPPENS, SO SEND THEM $$$!!)

#102: FINDING YOUR UMBRELLA AFTER LOSING IT MONTHS AGO...

..JUST IN TIME FOR THE WORST STORM ALL YEAR!!

YES!!

1-18

Panel 1: What's wrong, Gunth?
The city is gonna remove the billboard outside my bedroom window.

Panel 2: I pull my shades up every morning & find that billboard staring at me through the glass!!

Panel 3: It's like family to me.

Panel 4: Gunther's uncle & cousins are peeping Toms.

Panel 1: Gunther!! How is your billboard occupation going? Not so good.

Panel 2: How so? I forgot to bring food.

Panel 3: That might pose a problem. I forgot to bring water, too. OUCH.

Panel 4: I forgot I was afraid of heights, too. Didn't forget the cell phone, though.

Panel 1: GUNTHER'S BILLBOARD OCCUPATION: 14TH MINUTE. If the city tears down this billboard, what next? A ban on junk mail? No more product placement?

Panel 2: CORPORATE ADVERTISING SHAPED ME INTO THE MAN I AM TODAY!!

Panel 3: What a moron. If he doesn't stand for something, he'll fall for anything. That's what I'm hoping for.

▲The syndicate made me change the third panel. A gun firing is a no-no.

▲Another I was surprised went through.

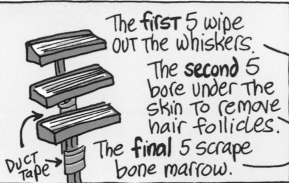

▲More Gunther abuse.

▲Ya gotta love the cheap wine at Trader Joe's.

THE OPPOSITE OF FAN-BOY

Mr. Knight. It is an honor to meet you.

I abhor your work.

You're a **HACK** & an embarrassment to your profession. The Red Sox stink. And your music is an abomination!!

I filled up two barf bags viewing your art exhibit. Expect them in your P.O. Box next week!!

Again, it was an honor to meet you.

May your drawing hand be bitten off by a jackal!!

I have met my Moriarty!!

▲This guy really exists! Haven't seen him in a while though.

MY ART OPENING

What'd you think?

Delectable!!

Rich, savory, eclectic. A delightful combination of light & heavy with an emphasis on fun!!

Wow!! I never heard my artwork described like that!!

I was talking about the hors d'oeuvres!!

BACK IN THE DAY

Hey kid!! I'll pay you five bucks a week to mow my lawn!!

Cool!!

RIGHT HERE RIGHT NOW

Hey kid!! I'll pay you twenty dollars a week to update my Facebook page!!

Forty!!

▲I only draw arms if necessary . . . The adult in the first panel looks weird, though.

2-1

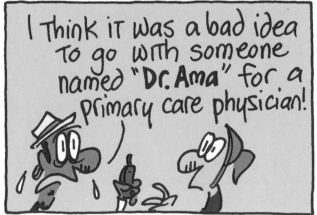

▲ "Dr. Ama" = drama. Some folks missed it.

▲I had to change this because you can't show puke on the comics page.

▲How do you sever an armpit?

THE EVIL THAT ROOMMATES DO

What's that smell?

My first shipment from the "Bacon of the Month" club.

sizzle crackle ss rs...

Oh no you didn't!!

Oh yes. Maple-cured, apple-smoked, Tequila-marinated, Thick-sliced foolishness.

sizzle ss crack

KEEF

Dude, you know I'm trying to give up meat!!

It's more fat than meat.

Salty, smoky fat...

smackle ss.

keef@knightlifecomic.com

Can you keep an eye on this pile of bacon whilst I go powder myself?

©2009 K. Knight/Dist. by UFS, Inc.

2-8

THIS CONCLUDES ANOTHER EPISODE OF: THE EVIL THAT ROOMMATES DO!!

AUGH!! MUNCH CRUNCH DEVOUR

www.comics.com

▲Mmmmmmmm. Bacon.

▲*God: A Memoir* would've never flown in many of the newspapers, so it was changed to *Genius: A Memoir*.

Barnaby, don't hate on the grade-schoolers who debunked your new memoir!!

It's **chock-full** of lies!! Your publisher should've never put this book out!!

GOD: A Memoir by Barnaby

2-12

How could your publisher believe that you supplied Jesse Owens with steroids during the 1936 Olympic Games?

"Barnaby Press" has declined to comment at this time.

KEEF

The worst part of my memoir being proven a fake is the dissolution of my development deal!!

I went from a multi-picture deal with the world's 2ND-largest movie company...

2-13

...To a multi-panel deal with a 3rd-rate newspaper cartoonist!! OUCH!!

KEEF

In honor of Louis Braille's 200TH birthday, I've let the acne grow on my face to ask you something.

Feel my forehead to see if you can figure it out!! Uh-oh.

I hope she doesn't expect me to pop the question.

KEEF

2-14

▲ I don't know what I was thinking when I came up with this. I'm clearly disturbed.

Know what drives me bananas? All these blogs praising "Keith" Ledger's performance in "The Dark Knight"!!

2-15

If these bloggers had any respect for him & his performance, they'd get his name right!!

KEEF

Maybe you shouldn't google your own name so much.

Maybe you should go play in traffic.

▲My all-time favorite Dad strip. Fits him to a tee.

▲I don't have anything against clowns, I sat next to one in second grade.

▲Hippies, mimes, Canadians, and Red Sox fans are the only people you can make fun of nowadays.

You were right about Madden '09, Gunther.

For years I thought it was all about duping folks into annually dropping **big bucks** for essentially the **same game** with a different cover.

www.comics.com

But I gotta admit, this new pre-game tailgate party feature is TOP-SHELF!!

There's some opposing team fans..Git 'em!!

I especially enjoy the 3 new types of steroids players can obtain.

Pick up that whizzinator over there.

keef@knightlifecomic.com

And, of course, the new cheerleader warm-ups.

Woof.

©2009 K. Knight/Dist. by UFS, Inc.

3-1

When do we play the actual football game?

Football? They dropped that part **YEARS** ago!!

KEEF

▲I can't believe I got away with "whizzinator."

▲The life coach is played by Kenny G.

▲ I received more accusations of being a racist.

OPEN MIC NIGHT

Hello. I'm Captain Giggles. I won't be doing my usual poetry.

I'm going to talk about layoffs, foreclosures, & economic uncertainty.

keef@knightlifecomic.com

No matter how bad things get, remember the great Howard Jones song, "Things can only get Better"!!

KEEF

I'm saying, cheer up!! As long as you have your health, family & friends, you'll be all right.
Thank you.

www.comics.com

Did we just receive a pep talk from Emo-boy?

I think so!!

We're DOOMED.

©2009 K. Knight/Dist. by UFS, Inc.

3-8

▲Captain Giggles is played by that guy in the Cure.

▲My character saying "Not what you think" was cut.

▲Joker in the restroom. C'mon!! Good stuff!!

▲More Gunther abuse.

▲This series connected with a lot of folks.

BRING AN UNEMPLOYED PARENT TO SCHOOL WEEK

Honey, I souped up your desk while you were at recess.

LAID OFF U.S. AUTO WORKER

!

It sits 4 feet higher than all other desks, has 3 times the storage room & seats eight!!

How will the students behind me see the board?

Who cares? This is the S.U.V. of desks!!

Yeah. Selfish, Unnecessary & Vain.

3-19

BRING YOUR UNEMPLOYED PARENT TO SCHOOL WEEK

I think we mixed this Kool-Aid incorrectly.

Looks fine to me!!

It burned a hole through the counter!!

Is that a bad thing?

FORMER FDA REGULATOR

3-20

BRING YOUR UNEMPLOYED PARENT TO SCHOOL WEEK

How'd we do on your science exam?

We flunked.

I don't see what's wrong with our answer.

The teacher wanted more than "God did it."

3-21

Life's LITTLE VICTORIES
DURING THE RECESSION!!

#1929: YOUR NEW APARTMENT IS ALREADY OUTFITTED WITH LONG-LASTING ECO-BULBS!!

www.comics.com

Yes!!

#1930: YOU EAT SO MANY FREE SAMPLES AT THE SUPERMARKET...

Meatballs!!

Baby Mushroom quiche

Wheat Pasta with garlic pesto

Organic Carrot juice!!

..THERE'S NO NEED TO COOK AT HOME!!

©2009 K. Knight/Dist. by UFS, Inc.

#1931: INSTEAD OF LAYING PEOPLE OFF...

Happy Long week-end!!

..YOUR COMPANY SWITCHES TO A FOUR-DAY WORK WEEK!!

#1932: YOUR APARTMENT BUILDING SETS UP A DVD/BOOK EXCHANGE IN THE LAUNDRY ROOM.

KILLER CLOWNS from OUTER SPACE?!!
Yes!!
3-22

Take One Leave One

#1933: YOUR FAVORITE AUTHOR DOES A FREE READING AT THE LOCAL LIBRARY!!

COMPLETE K CHRONICLES

▲It's "Killer Klowns." How could I mess up another K.K. name?

SEND YOUR LITTLE VICTORIES TO:
keef@knightlifecomic.com !!

LIBRARY SEMINAR: SURVIVING THE NEW DEPRESSION

Don't sit around expecting to be bailed out!! Be proactive!!

Do you have the intestinal fortitude to make it through these hard times?

I had intestinal fortitude once. Horrible. From a taco stand in Tijuana.

3-23

Are you the new courtroom sketch artist?

That's me!!

A few of us have been reviewing the work you're doing on the corporate fraud case.

3-24

None of us recall the defendants having devil horns or forked tongues.

Are any of you paying attention?

Your weird, opinionated courtroom sketches are a hit on our website.

COURTHOUSE

Management is assigning you 3 more trials & a bunch of other stuff.

3-25

Is there something wrong with your eyes?

RUB RUB

Oh, I see.

▲I drew caricatures in Boston's Faneuil Hall all through college.

▲I was called an evil, racist !@#$% for this one. Dedicated to all the black butlers and maids.

GUESS WHO LOST IN A GAME OF PICTIONARY?

OHMIGOSH!! We Beat a Real, Live Cartoonist!!

www.comics.com

NEEDLESS TO SAY, MY "FRIENDS" WERE RUBBING IT IN.

We're NURSES!! And WE BEAT YOU at PICTIONARY!!

DEJECTED, I SOUGHT SOLACE IN THE STREETS

Had a cousin named Clifford who was a detective...

KEEF

..ended up losing to his 6-year-old in a game of CLUE...

The next day he jumped in front of a STEAMROLLER.

©2009 K. Knight/Dist. by UFS, Inc.

Don't sweat it, kid. It's just a game.

You're right!! I'm an ADULT!! Mature!! I'm gonna go back there & take this loss like a MAN!!

3-29

INSTEAD, I KICKED THEIR BUTTS IN OPERATION!!

KEITH!! I've been looking all over for you!!

I want to interview a highly skilled & respected cartoonist for my public access TV show!!

So I thought I'd ask you!!

WOW!! Thanks for the--

Do you have the phone number of the guy who draws Candorville?

▲ A tip o' the pen to comrade in arms, Darrin Bell.

What should I wear for my TV interview?

Don't bother!!

Why?

The show web site sez "Nothing Left On" gets local artists, poets & writers to bare all.

Heh...I'm sure they mean that figuratively.

I don't think so.

Sez here it's been re-NUDE for next season!!

I didn't know you did your show in the all-together!!

What did you expect from a show called "Nothing Left on"?

I don't want to do a TV interview with no clothes!!

Think of all the exposure you'll be getting!!

▲ "Angela" is a shout-out to activist Angela Davis.

▲ I especially appreciate snail-mail from jail!!

▲This strip didn't make it through, so you're seeing it for the first time.

4-12

▲The zookeeper has five fingers in the second panel, four fingers in the fourth. A finger was bitten off between panels!!

Why the "Thriller" outfit?

Michael Jackson is having an auction this week.

For those who cannot afford his High-priced kitsch, I will be selling my Michael Jackson impersonator stuff out on the street for cheap!!

Will you finally toss the Jheri-curl moisturizer in the medicine cabinet?

Certain things I can never part with!!

▲ It's 1,000,000% true! I was a teenaged Michael Jackson impersonator!!

4-20

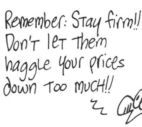

SELLING OFF MY MICHAEL JACKSON STUFF

I'm off!! Wish me luck!!

=smack=

Good luck!!

Remember: Stay firm!! Don't let them haggle your prices down too much!!

DON'T STOP 'TIL YOU GET ENOUGH!!

4-21

SELLING OFF MY MICHAEL JACKSON STUFF

I have a question about this "Beat it" jacket.

Shoot.

BILL

Is this real leather?

What kind of question is that?!! I was **THE TOP** Michael Jackson impersonator in my High school!!

That's 110% imitation leather, honey!!

BILL

4-22

▲ As of press time, the wifey is ahead by one broken glass.

You're selling what?

Mexican Coca-Cola!! It's way better than the U.S. version!!

CAFE

IT comes in glass bottles!! It has **real** sugar instead of high-fructose corn syrup!! You can really taste the difference!!

4-27

Wow. That is good.

I only need to sell 12 cases to pay for the ones I've already consumed!!

ON THE PHONE WITH DAD

Find any extra work yet?

I'm helping my neighbor sell cases of Coca-Cola he brings back from Tijuana.

4-28

You're in cahoots with a low-level Mexican Coke smuggler?

Yeah. I suppose I am.

Good!! Now I don't have to lie to my friends about what you do for a living!!

Okay, babe. We're off to pick up more Mexican Coke!!

Be careful.

Gunther, is it really worth going over the border for a case of soda?

We're not really going. It's just for show!!

4-29

What do you mean?

I get my supply from a taqueria 3 blocks away!!

▲I was going to make the "babe" in the first panel Gunther's mom, but it would've been too creepy.

▲All the schools in the strip are named after black actors from the seventies.

I think the police officer I'm riding with is an imposter!!

Problem is, he's the best partner I've had in years!! I don't know what to do!!

You pulled me over just to tell me this? I can search your vehicle if you want.

Is that him? Yup. Whaddaya think? Too young?

I'd say the lollipop gives him away. What?!! Haven't you ever seen Kojak?

The department discovered that my partner for the past few months was a toddler.

As absurd as it seems, that little kid taught me more about my job than any of my superiors!! How so?

He showed me that if I approach policing with the enthusiasm of a child, I will be a more effective peace officer. Nice one.

And wearing a diaper eliminates pesky bathroom breaks during stakeouts. Right on.

We got our COBRA application in the mail.

COBRA?!! DON'T OPEN IT!!

COBRA is a privately funded terrorist organization whose rise in the 1980s--

--was thwarted by a group of real American heroes: G.I. JOE!!

COBRA is a federal law that allows us to keep our health insurance after being laid off.

Sounds like a plot by Destro.

5-10

There's something wriggling in the envelope.

Ooo!! Now I'm curious!!

KEEF

▲Kerstin quit wearing her Red Sox cap because she didn't know how to respond to "!@*& Yeah!"

WEDDING ANNOUNCEMENTS (FOR THE REST OF US)

Ryan Chadwick & Miriam Ty met at a pawn shop where both were selling the same brand of guitar. They now share one guitar & each other.

Kim Gilliam & Rod Innes were both fired from their jobs by e-mail the day they were to meet, courtesy of an Internet dating service.

Tyler Watkins & Nillie Graham exchanged numbers after running into each other one too many times eating free samples at Costco.

▲The *New York Times* wedding announcements fascinate and repulse me.

▲C'mon!! Who else would mention Joy Division in a daily comic strip?

▲I was gonna throw a can of Pepsi in there but thought it too obscure.

▲Shout-out to Charles Schulz.

▲Kerstin does this and thinks it's funny.

▲Someone at Lucasfilm told me my strips are hanging up all over the place in their cubicles.

Revenge of *Life's Little Victories*

#100: SWITCHING FROM THE **SMUT CHANNEL** TO THE **OPRAH CHANNEL** JUST BEFORE YOUR SPOUSE WALKS IN!!

OOH!! A JANE AUSTEN FILM!!

Why of course!!

#101: BEATING THE GUY WHO BRINGS HIS OWN POOL STICK TO THE LOCAL PUB!!

YES!!

HA!! SUCKER!!

#102: RECEIVING PROPS FOR A SHIRT YOU SCORED IN THE 99¢ BIN!!

Nice!! DOLCE & Gabbana?

Debbie Gibson.

#103: RUSHING TO DUMP AN OVERSTUFFED TRASH BAG BEFORE IT RIPS...

GAANNGWAAAY

..AND IT **BURSTS** JUST AS YOU REACH THE GARBAGE CAN!!

YES!!

RIIIP!!!

KEEF

©2009 K. Knight/Dist. by UFS, Inc.

www.comics.com

5-31

▲ "The Banana Slugs" is the nickname for the sports teams at U.C. Santa Cruz.

I heard dat yer callin' da balls-n-strikes at today's game.

I'm Vinnie. I sponsor one of the peewee baseball teams playing today.

Shake!!

6-4

Can I flush & wash my hands first?

Did I catch you at an awkward time?

MEN

I'm the sponsor of the peewee baseball team in the visitor's dugout.

My kid's pitchin', & if you rub my back, I'll rub yours... Here's my card.

"Vinnie's Thai massage parlor."

Funny. You don't look Thai.

I grew up in the Little Italy section of Bangkok.

6-5

How's your umpire gig going?

The game hasn't started.

But several parents have made questionable offers in an attempt to curry favor.

Have they made threats?

Nah. Just a little overzealous, that's all.

DEAD MAN WALKING!!

That's my cue. I gotta go.

KEEF

6-6

▲I really umpired once. I was accused of pulling for the team with the black kid on it.

I'm off to the all-natural beauty shop.

Can you pick up another peach melba loofah scrub?

YOU use my peach melba loofah scrub?

It leaves my skin silky smooth!! A lot of folks have been noticing!!

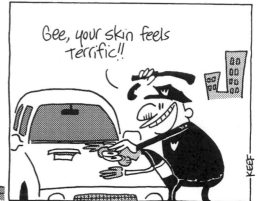

Gee, your skin feels terrific!!

$10 for a bar of soap?!!

HEALTHY & WELL
GREEN/ORGANIC BEAUTY
SPA

Ugh-- I know....

I can't afford anything in here, even with my employee discount!!

To shop at Healthy & Well, you've got to be wealthy as heck!!

So why is all this wellness stuff so expensive?

One reason is we do not test our products on animals!!

How does that make it more expensive?

It ain't cheap getting prisons to loan us the Wall St. execs!!

AIEEE

▲Wall Street execs are the new go-to villains.

▲When will Shields and Yarnell make a comeback?

▲I can imagine how strange it would be to start reading the strip with this one.

▲Always been fascinated by maggots.

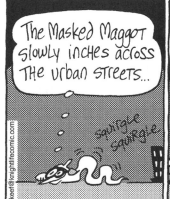

Dearest.. I'd like to talk to you about the return of "M.M."

Marshall Mathers?

You know who I mean!! "She who strikes fear & nausea in the hearts & minds of all who encounter her!!"

You realize Marilyn Manson is a guy, right?

6-25

KEEF

Ever since I told my wife that my bike got stolen, the street vigilante, "Masked Maggot," has returned.

I don't know who she's tryin' to fool. Everyone in the neighborhood knows who it is.

Wait a sec..

You know who the Masked Maggot is?

You're joking, right?

Is it Jada Pinkett Smith?

6-26

Maybe the Clark Kent/Superman thing ain't so far-fetched after all!!

Is it Katie Couric?

KEEF

The MASKED MAGGOT!! Thank goodness you're here!!

How can I help?

I have this **festering wound** from a lower back tattoo gone wrong. Could you eat away at the infected area?

I do believe we have moved beyond the Masked Maggot's payscale!

6-27

KEEF

Why is there a slice of bacon taped to your arm?

It's my meat patch.

It's the newest late-nite infomercial sensation!!

After 3 days, a scab forms over the slice. After 5, it gets absorbed into the bloodstream, satisfying all my meat needs!!

KEEF

That's the most revolting thing I've ever heard!!

But it works, bra.

You know I love bacon. Yet I haven't had the urge to eat this slice here... And it's been **two** days!!

Gotta give you props for that.

The 37 slices that were stuck to my belly are a different story.

6-28

▲Easiest strip I ever had to draw.

BENEATH
THE VALLEY
OF THE
**LIFE'S
LITTLE
VICTORIES!!**

#628: ARRIVING TO WORK AFTER **SKIPPING BREAKFAST**...

GRUMBLE grumble

..AND FINDING **BAGELS** IN THE STAFF LOUNGE!!

Yes!!

7-5

#629: RECEIVING **FREE PASSES** TO A NEW FILM...

AWAY ~~WE GO~~

=sniff=

excellent.

AND IT ROCKS!!

KEEF

#630: PICKING UP A **BASKETBALL** FOR THE FIRST TIME IN **YEARS**...

Yes!!

PAF!

..AND HITTING A 20-FOOTER!!

www.comics.com

#631: BUYING A $5 BURRITO

LUNCH DINNER BREAKFAST

AND IT LASTS FOR **3 MEALS!!**

#632: WALKING THROUGH A **SKETCHY** PART OF TOWN..

Uh... Yes?

Whoozat?

AND PEOPLE ARE AFRAID OF **YOU!**

▲ I wanna own a minor league baseball or hockey team when I grow up.

MY GERMAN WIFE ENCOUNTERS SAUERKRAUT AT THE BALLPARK

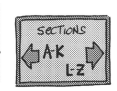

SECTIONS
◀ A-K
L-Z ▶

FREE?!! ARE YOU SERIOUS?

Yup. For the hot dogs.

DUMP

7-9

You don't have to eat it all now. It's free the whole game!!

That's crazy talk!!

▲ Sauerkraut is good for regularity.

MINOR LEAGUE BASEBALL

EXIT

I've seen people tossed out of ballgames for drinking too much..

For running onto the field & interrupting play...

PARKING LOT

7-10

BUT I never thought I'd witness someone being tossed for eating too much free sauerkraut!!

I got the last laugh--I snuck a jar out under my shirt!!

The toilet paper is located just past our in-house stock trader's office.

And the beach towels are in aisle six, across from the real estate desk.

Thanks!!

7-11

The 99¢ store has a lot more stuff than it used to!!

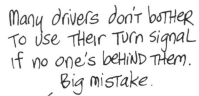

TALK RADIO CALL

I don't use my turn signal because I don't want **THE MAN** To know where I'm going!!

Next thing you know, The government will be demanding a daily itinerary from me!!

AND PRETTY SOON, PEOPLE WILL BE MARRYING GOATS!!

You've mixed up your Talking points, ma'am.

What's up, Gunther?

Someone posted a fake Facebook profile about me!!

Oh my goodness!! What are you doing about it?

I'm gonna ask me To be my friend!! I sound really cool!!

Gunth, I heard someone set up a fake Facebook profile about you.

Yeah, It's got 25,000 friends!!

It sez I'm a **Peruvian folk hero**.. That I cavort with **supermodels**.. & That I invented **ice**!!

Celebrities & royalty are begging to be "friended"!!

I'm gonna link This fake profile to my web site & milk it for all it's worth!!

Tap Tap

I never knew I was such a fun guy!!

Did he say "fungi"?

▲ Shout-outs to Biggie, Flavor Flav, and Sir Mix-a-Lot all in one strip!

The Ciggy Smalls "Smoking Gun" ad campaign was named worst ad of the 20th century by Business Weak.

7-23

"The ad consisted of me pointing two pistols with lit cigarettes sticking out of the barrels."...

GET SMOKED!!

Ciggy Smalls

But if you noticed, the ads **never** showed me actually smoking!!

Of course!! Ya don't wanna be a bad influence on the kids!!

KEEF

Did you know that cigarette butts make up 30% of all litter?

Not one of those butts was ever a Ciggy Smalls!!

Smokers of Ciggy Smalls can redeem their butts for fabulous prizes from this catalog!!

7-24

500 butts earns you an iron lung.

20 butts gets you yellow teeth!!

KEEF

HANSEL UND GRETEL

Hansel!! The birds ate all the bread crumbs!! Now we'll never find our way home!!

Don't worry, Gretel!! I've been dropping cigarette butts!!

Do you think they'll help us get home?

Sure!! Just follow the dead birds!!

How are the comics my brother sent from Germany?

Weird, like those tiny bathing trunks he wears.

DER COMIX

7-25

KEEF

VET MENTORING

A guy in my unit smothered an IED -- took one for the team.

When I got home, I went to tell his loved ones what kind of sacrifice he made.

Turns out he was gay!! I was the first one to let his partner know what happened!!

I've shared things with soldiers that I'd **never** tell family & friends. War does that.

Here was a guy who gave his **life** for his fellow soldiers.. but wasn't allowed to share with us who was waiting for him back home!!

If we're not fighting for this soldier's freedom-- Then what are we fighting for?

©2009 K. Knight/Dist. by UFS, Inc.

7-26

KEEF

www.comics.com

▲ I got several e-mails and letters from people saying they changed their minds about "Don't ask/Don't tell" just from reading this strip.

It's true! If it weren't for bullies, I wouldn't be where I am today. ▲

▲An homage to '80s sci-fi classic *The Highlander*.

▲ MJ: R.I.P.

BOSTON FOR MY BIRTHDAY!!

What are you looking forward to most about flying back east?

Hmmm...Lessee: Lobster Rolls, decent pizza, fried clams, steak & cheese subs...

Pistachio Ice Cream, Dunkin' Donuts coffee, Scorpion Bowls...

I noticed you didn't mention any family or friends.

Who?

Here we are!! Malden, Mass!! My hometown!!

ENTERING MALDEN

Birthplace of Converse All-Stars, Jack Albertson of "Chico & The Man," and Van Halen's greatest singer, Gary Cherone!!

THE SQUIRE

Because of its close proximity to Boston, affordability & low crime, BusinessWeek named Malden THE **best place** to raise a kid in Massachusetts!!

Would **YOU** raise a kid here?

Are you **NUTS?!!** Look what an ingrate I turned out to be!!

▲The Squire (2nd panel) is a strip joint located near the Malden/Revere, MA line.

BOSTON 4 MY BIRTHDAY!!

I got sick in this parking lot after a Sox game when I was a kid!!

GAME DAY PARKING

I woke up in my underpants in a ditch after hitting this nightclub back in my college days!!

I saw a rat **THIS BIG** coming outta this subway station!!

T

I would've preferred to walk the Freedom Trail!!

▲Kelly's Roast Beast: Best lobster roll in the greater Boston area.

▲Shout-out to my fellow S.S.C. grad & "Off the Mark" creator, Mark Parisi.

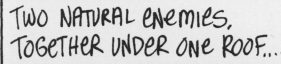

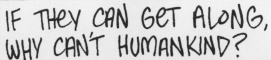

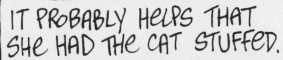

▲My uncle Owen passed a few weeks after this strip ran. I'm glad he got to see it.

▲Ugh. I regret this one.

About the Author

Cartoonist Keith Knight is the hardest-working man in the comics business.

Keith Knight is the creator of three comic strips; the nationally syndicated auto-bio daily, *The Knight Life*, the award-winning alternative weekly strip, *The K Chronicles*, and the single-panel social/political commentary panel, *(th)ink*.

Born and raised in the Boston area, Keith Knight was weaned on a steady diet of Star Wars, hip-hop, racism, and Warner Bros. cartoons. He's been drawing comics since grade school. After graduating from college with a degree in graphic design, Knight drove out to San Francisco in the early '90s. It was in the Bay Area where Knight developed his trademark cartooning style that has been described as a cross between *Calvin & Hobbes* and underground comix.

Knight is part of a new generation of talented young African-American artists who infuse their work with urgency, edge, humor, satire, politics, and race. His art has appeared in various publications worldwide, including Salon.com, *ESPN the Magazine*, *L.A. Weekly*, *MAD Magazine*, the *Funny Times*, and *World War 3 Illustrated*. Knight also won the 2007 Harvey Award and the 2006, 2007, and 2008 Glyph Awards for Best Comic Strip. Three of his comix were the basis for an award-winning live-action short film, *Jetzt Kommt Ein Karton*, in Germany. His comic art has appeared in museums and galleries from San Francisco (CA) to Angoulême (France).

Keith's work has been collected in nine books so far: seven collections of his multi-panel strip, *The K Chronicles*, and two collections of single-panel strips and *(th)ink* anthologies titled *Red, White, Black & Blue* and most recently *Are We Feeling Safer Yet?* He also co-wrote and illustrated *The Beginner's Guide to Community-Based Art*.

His semi-conscious hip-hop band, the Marginal Prophets, will kick your ass. Their second disc, *Bohemian Rap CD*, won the California Music Award for Outstanding Rap Album, beating out rap heavyweights Paris, Aceyalone, E-40, Too-Short, and Ice Cube's Westside Connection. Hip-hop music with a punk-rock aesthetic.

Keith Knight is available to perform his hilarious and inspirational multi-media comic strip show at your university, high school, library, community center, or church. For more details, contact the artist at keef@kchronicles.com.